GROWTH COMPANION JOURNAL

90 DAYS
OF BECOMING!

A Special Gift for:

....

NOTE FROM THE AUTHOR

In between the hustle of paying the bills, completing school assignments, making sure there's food on the table, and just the daily quest to fulfil our obligations — we tend to forget our true life's calling.

With this journal, you can simply have fun discovering what's core to your life's purpose — as you take deliberate actions towards the accomplishment of your dreams. Enjoy it!

-KAMBY KAMARA-

HOW TO USE THIS JOURNAL

- Say your Affirmation with confidence

- List 10 things you are grateful for

- Write out your Life's Mission/Vision and Why it's important to you

- List your personal values

- List things you must confront and those you must embrace

- Look through the Goals List and pick a goal to achieve in the next 90 Days

- Write down your Bucket and Wish list

- Follow a Morning Power Routine *(Use the daily checklist included to start your day with a boost of energy and flow)*

- Set your target for the week and list your action plans for the day

- Record your most dominant mood for each day

- At the end of the week, review and record how many days you've been happy or sad. *(This will help you keep track of your emotional and mental wellbeing)*

- List the targets won (Highlight your progress and keep as a record of accomplishments)

- List your REWARD *(Celebrate your efforts to build positive momentum)*

- Use the Thoughts and Emotions pages to record how you feel, prayers, affirmations and more.

AFFIRMATION

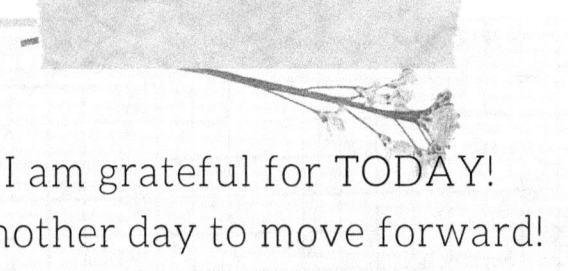

I am grateful for TODAY! Another day to move forward! The next 90 days are going to be so exciting and powerful because I am ADVANCING.

I am finding my true place in life. I see myself doing the things I love with the right people, at the right time, at the right place, earning good MONEY.

Right here, right now, I am experiencing divine favour, perfect health, love, peace, protection, happiness, success, abundance, and PROSPERITY!

Thank You, ... for being the source of my SUPPLY!

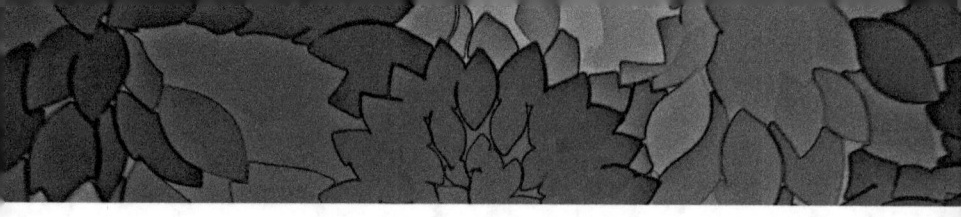

10 THINGS I'M GRATEFUL FOR!

Gratitude for what you have right now will inspire
your vision to create the next beautiful thing.

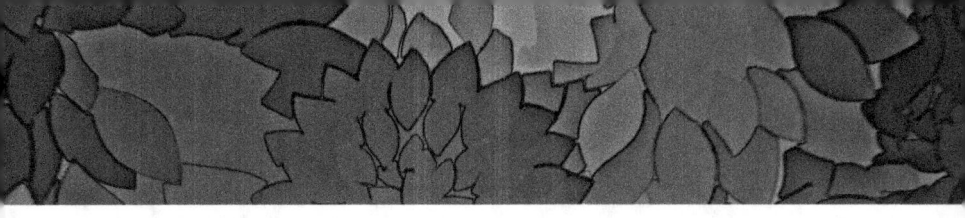

Keep being grateful...!

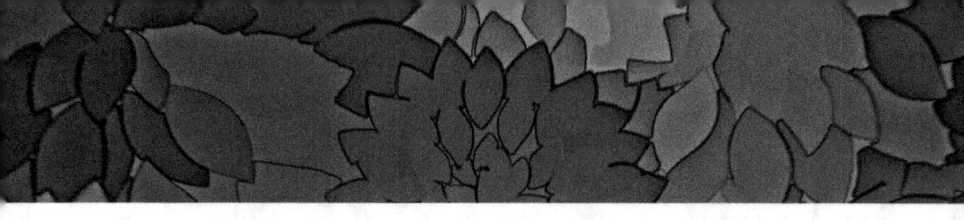

LIFE MISSION/VISION

What calls out to you? What product, service or contribution do you want to create as your gift to humanity?

_____
_____
_____
_____
_____
_____
_____
_____
_____
_____
_____
_____
_____
_____
_____
_____
_____
_____
_____
_____

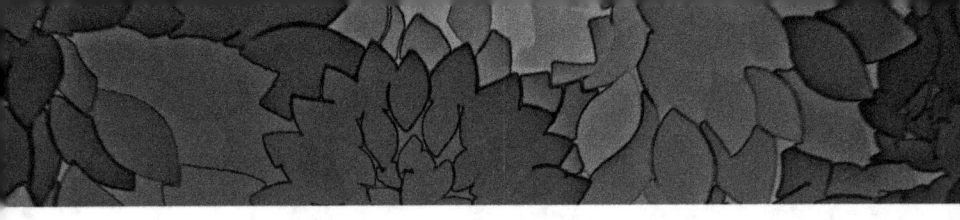

WHY?

Why is it important for you to actualise this vision? What good will it bring to yourself and the universe?

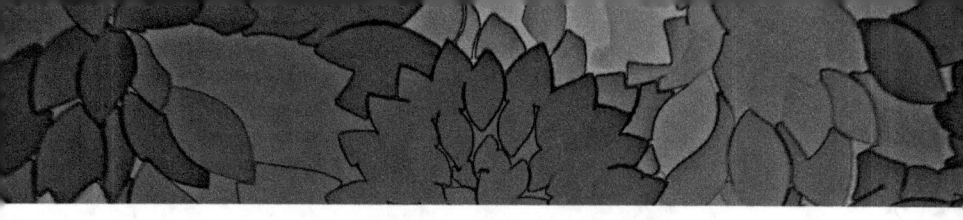

PERSONAL VALUES

Your values will determine your boundaries! What do you value most in life? List five(5) core traits and qualities you seek in yourself and others — E.g. Honesty, Clear Communication, etc

3.

4.

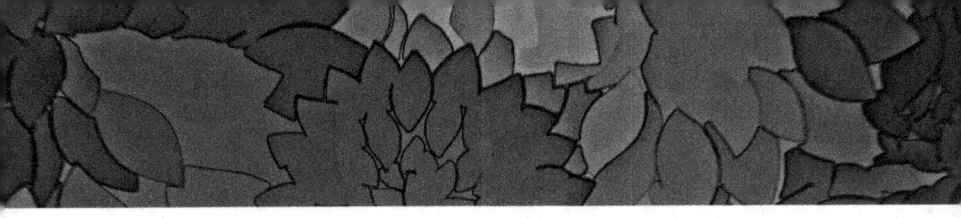

OPPOSITIONS TO CONFRONT

List the old habits, attitudes, beliefs, or toxic relationships you need to challenge, manage or let go of now — to become your best self.

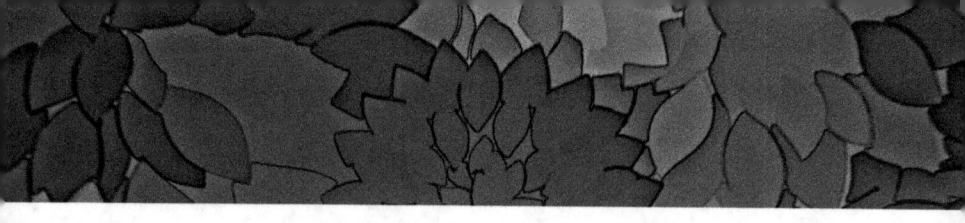

ALLIES TO EMBRACE

List the new concepts/ideas, attitudes, habits or relationships you need to embrace to create the life you desire.

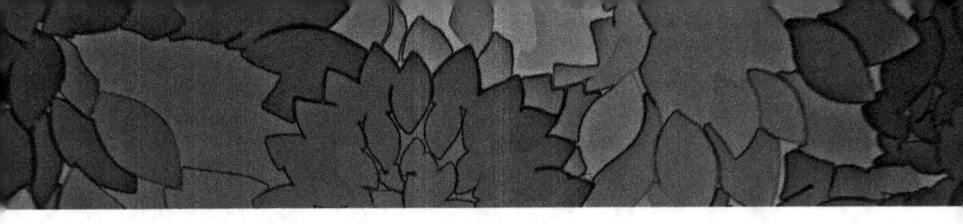

OTHER

What else do you want to add?

MY GOALS LIST

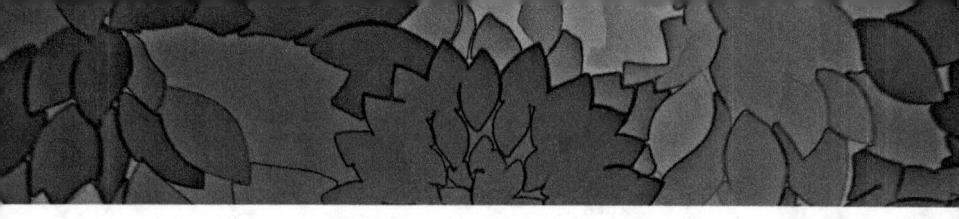

GOALS LIST

Chose the most EXCITING goal you would love to accomplish in the next 90 DAYS!

1. Intellectual and Spiritual Development
2. Body and Nutrition
3. Emotional and Mental Health
4. Personal Development (Self-Love)
5. Image and Personality
6. Talent and Skill Development
7. Family and Friends
8. Love Relationship
9. Study/Educational Development
10. Career Advancement
11. Business/Self-Employment
12. Money and Financial Investment
13. Networking/Connections
14. Community/National Development
15. Politics and Governance
16. Possessions /Material Wealth
17. Travel/Explore/Play

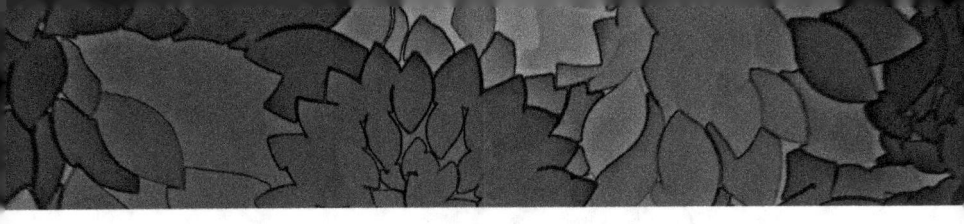

INTELLECTUAL & SPIRITUAL

How can you increase your knowledge and understanding about life and how it works? E.g. books, videos etc. #Enlightenment

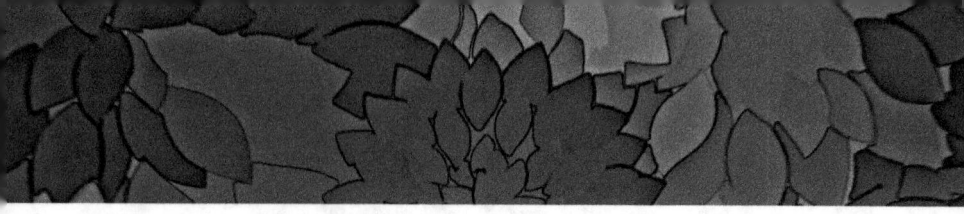

BODY & NUTRITION

How do you intend to become the most healthy and absolutely vibrant version of yourself? E.g. Exercise & Veggies

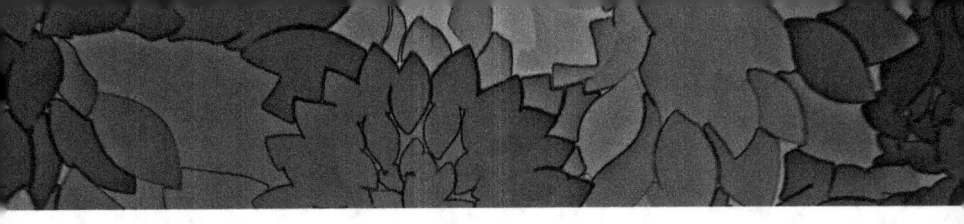

EMOTIONAL & MENTAL HEALTH

Your health is valuable! How can you nurture, protect and improve your emotional and mental wellbeing?

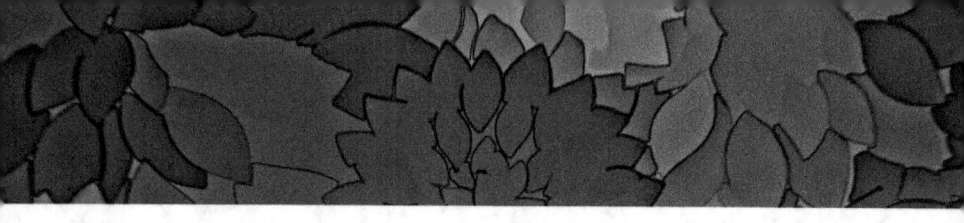

PERSONAL DEVELOPMENT (SELF-LOVE)

What is that aching desire that you'd love to manifest for your own happiness and personal growth?

_____

_____

_____

_____

_____

_____

_____

_____

_____

_____

_____

_____

_____

_____

_____

_____

_____

_____

_____

_____

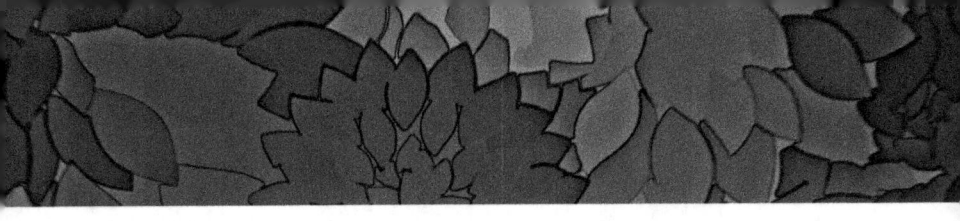

IMAGE & PERSONALITY

How do you want to be perceived ? What self image do you want to express to the world? Eg. Wardrobe - #Swag

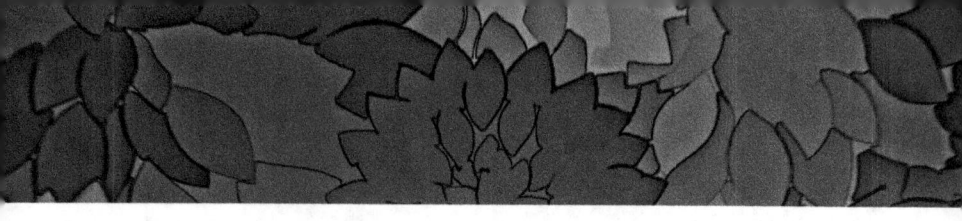

TALENT & SKILL DEVELOPMENT

What talents and skills do you have? How can you use and turn them into tangible and valuable assets? Eg. Cooking, Hairdressing, etc.

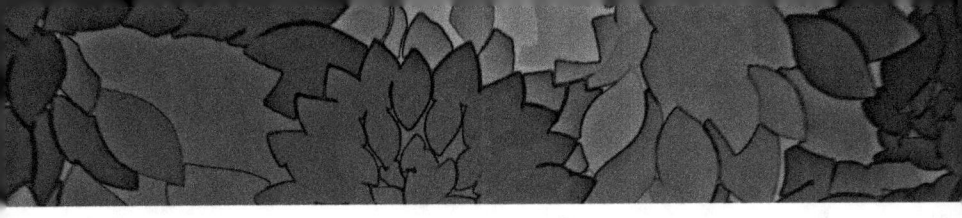

FAMILY & FRIENDS

How do you intend to stay connected with your family and friends?
What colourful memories do you want to create with them?

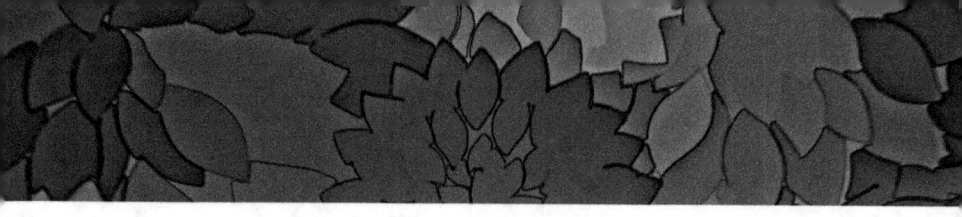

LOVE RELATIONSHIP

What relationship skills do you lack? What must you learn now to begin to design a stable, yet passionate love connection?

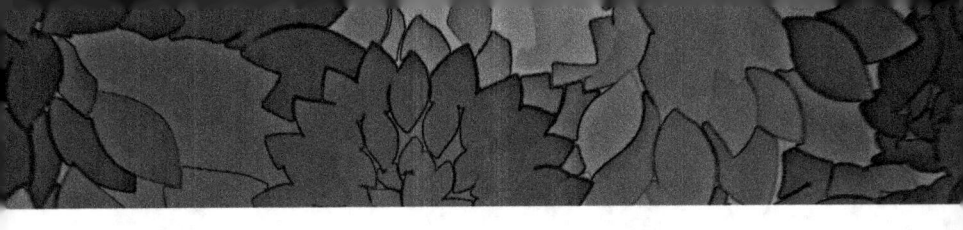

CAREER ADVANCEMENT

What must you do now to advance in your career or increase your chances for growth and expansion?

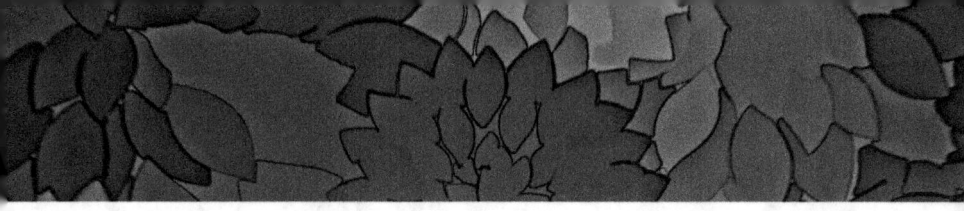

MONEY & FINANCIAL INVESTMENT

How can you positively increase the flow of MONEY in your bank accounts?

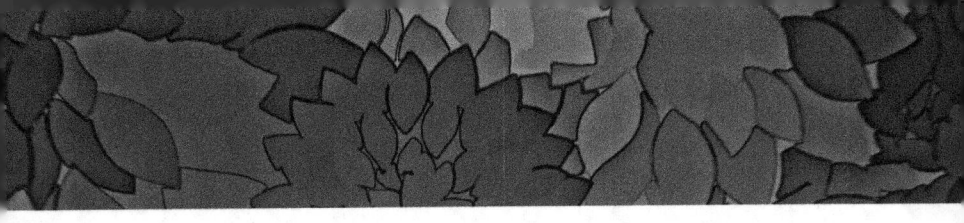

BUSINESS/SELF-EMPLOYMENT

How do you intend to start, grow and scale your business right now?

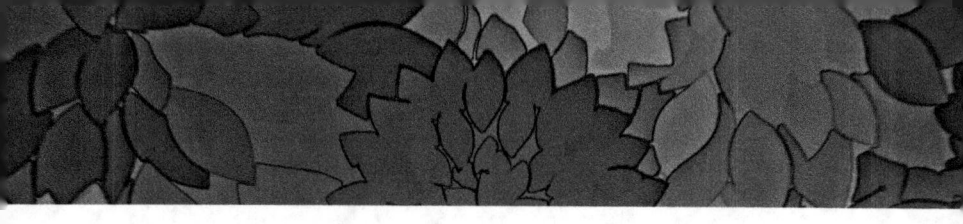

NETWORKING/CONNECTIONS

Who do you want to meet and connect with?
How can you be of mutual value to them?

_____
_____
_____
_____
_____
_____
_____
_____
_____
_____
_____
_____
_____
_____
_____
_____
_____
_____
_____
_____

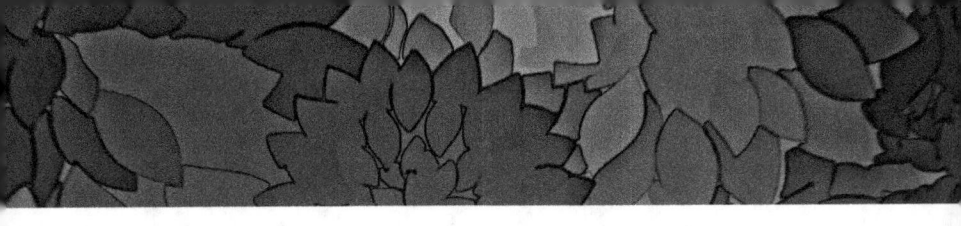

COMMUNITY/NATIONAL DEVELOPMENT

What needed PRODUCT or SERVICE would you love to develop as your contribution to your Community or Nation? #Giveback

_____
_____
_____
_____
_____
_____
_____
_____
_____
_____
_____
_____
_____
_____
_____
_____
_____
_____
_____
_____

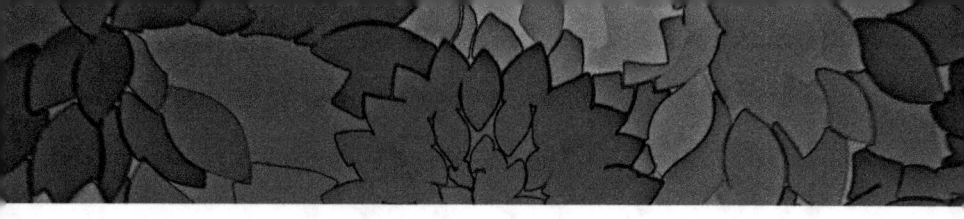

POLITICS & GOVERNANCE

What issues in politics and governance are you greatly unhappy about? What are you going to do about it?

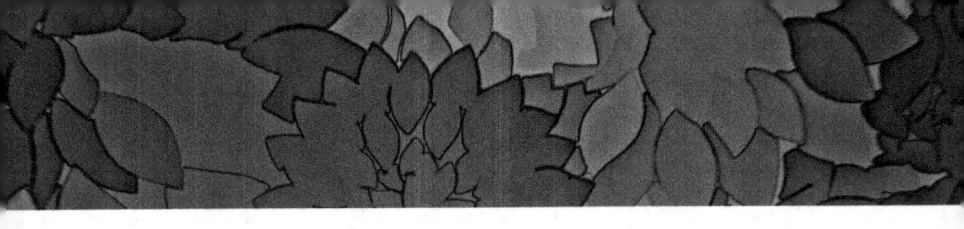

POSSESSIONS/MATERIAL WEALTH

What would you love to own right now as an outward manifestation of your inner wealth and prosperity?

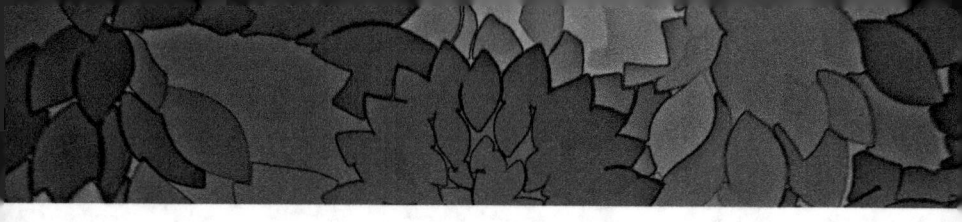

TRAVEL/EXPLORE/PLAY

Where do you want to go? What do you want to see?
Can you start by exploring where you are now?
Go—Discover—Connect—Play—Have Fun!

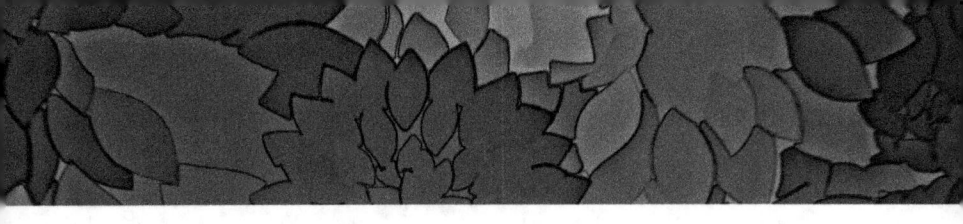

OTHER GOALS

What else do you want to do, be or have?

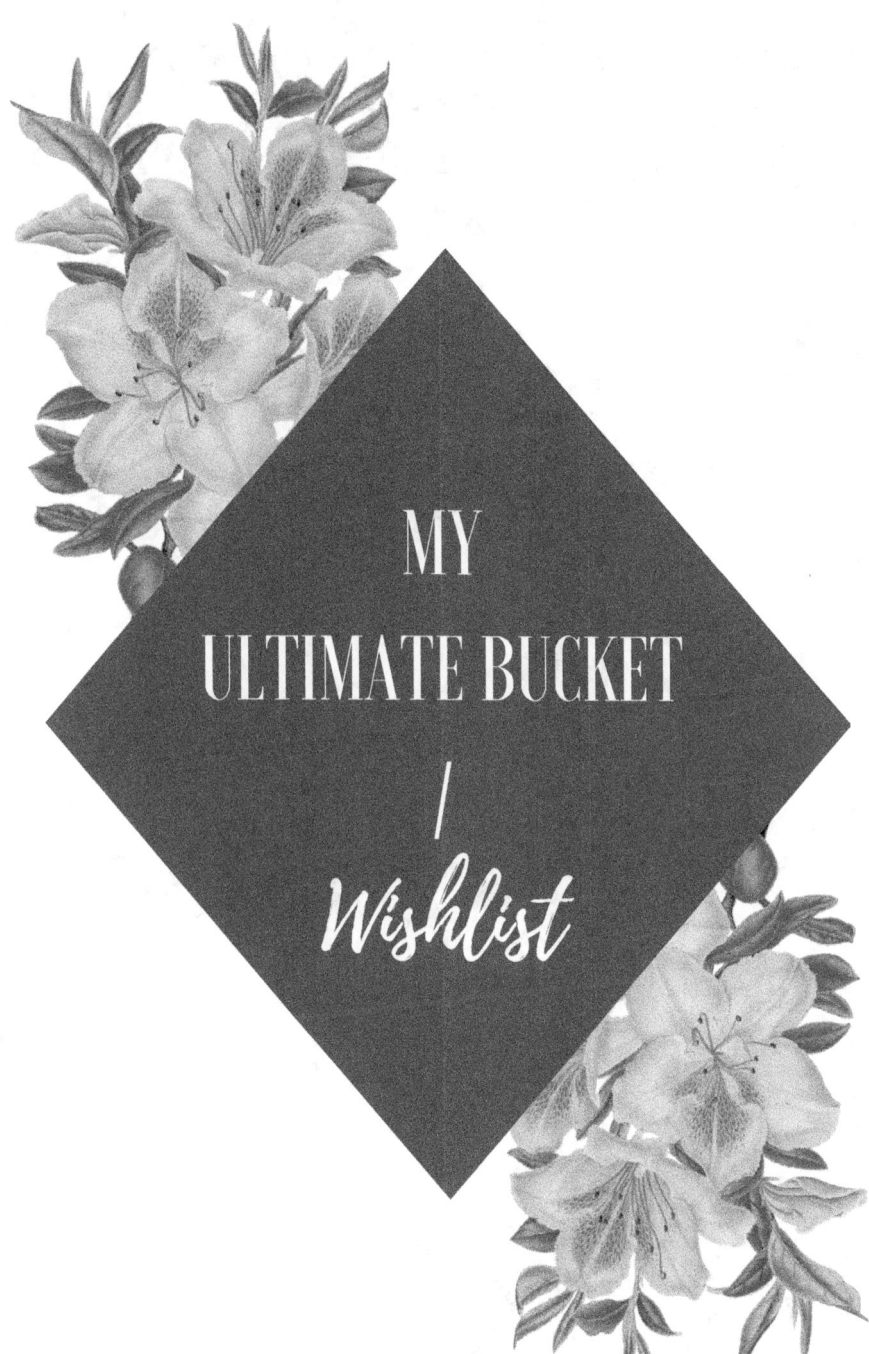

Bucketlist
E.g. Horse riding, Bungee jumping, etc.

Wishlist

ACCESSORIES:

BEAUTY:

BOOKS:

CLOTHES:

GADGETS:

SKINCARE:

90 DAYS

DAY	1	2	3	4	5	6	7	8	9	10	11	12	13	14
WAKE UP HAPPY AND BREATHE…	✓													
DRINK A GLASS OF WARM WATER														
AFFIRM/PRAY MEDITATE														
READ/REVIEW GOALS														
LIST ACTION PLANS														
EXERCISE														
OTHER														

DAY	29	30	31	32	33	34	35	36	37	38	39	40	41	42
WAKE UP HAPPY AND BREATHE…														
DRINK A GLASS OF WARM WATER														
AFFIRM/PRAY MEDITATE														
READ/REVIEW GOALS														
LIST ACTION PLANS														
EXERCISE														
OTHER														

OF BECOMING!

15	16	17	18	19	20	21	22	23	24	25	26	27	28	
														WAKE UP HAPPY AND BREATHE...
														DRINK A GLASS OF WARM WATER
														AFFIRM/PRAY MEDITATE
														READ/REVIEW GOALS
														LIST ACTION PLANS
														EXERCISE
														OTHER

43	44	45	46	47	48	49	50	51	52	53	54	55	56	
														WAKE UP HAPPY AND BREATHE...
														DRINK A GLASS OF WARM WATER
														AFFIRM/PRAY MEDITATE
														READ/REVIEW GOALS
														LIST ACTION PLANS
														EXERCISE
														OTHER

90 DAYS

DAY	57	58	59	60	61	62	63	64	65	66	67	68	69	70
WAKE UP HAPPY AND BREATHE...	✓													
DRINK A GLASS OF WARM WATER														
AFFIRM/PRAY MEDITATE														
READ/REVIEW GOALS														
LIST ACTION PLANS														
EXERCISE														
OTHER														

DAY	85	86	87	88	89	90
WAKE UP HAPPY AND BREATHE...						
DRINK A GLASS OF WARM WATER						
AFFIRM/PRAY MEDITATE						
READ/REVIEW GOALS						
LIST ACTION PLANS						
EXERCISE						
OTHER						

OF BECOMING!

71	72	73	74	75	76	77	78	79	80	81	82	83	84	
														WAKE UP HAPPY AND BREATHE...
														DRINK A GLASS OF WARM WATER
														AFFIRM/PRAY MEDITATE
														READ/REVIEW GOALS
														LIST ACTION PLANS
														EXERCISE
														OTHER

Trust Your Intuition!

Week 1

"Trust your Intuition
Trust the concept of Prayer
You do KNOW what to do!"

TARGET FOR THE WEEK

Less is more...!

ACTION PLANS

DAY 1 _____ *Date*
         M T W T F S S
_____
_____
_____
_____
_____

MOOD CHECK: Cloudy? ☐ *OR Happy?* ☐

DAY 2 _____ *Date*
M T W T F S S

_____

_____
_____
_____
_____

MOOD CHECK: *Cloudy?* ☐ *OR* *Happy?* ☐

DAY 3 _____ *Date*
M T W T F S S

_____

_____
_____
_____
_____

MOOD CHECK: *Cloudy?* ☐ *OR* *Happy?* ☐

DAY 4 _____ *Date*
M T W T F S S

_____

_____
_____
_____
_____

MOOD CHECK: *Cloudy?* ☐ *OR* *Happy?* ☐

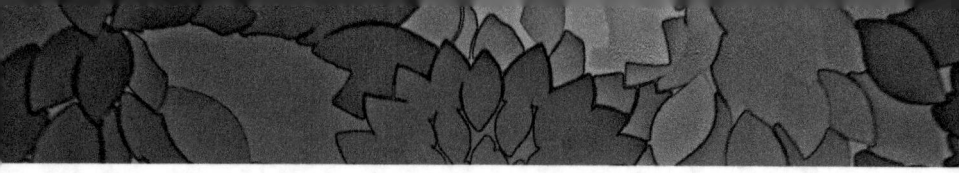

DAY 5 ———————————— *Date*
M T W T F S S

MOOD CHECK: *Cloudy?* ☐ OR *Happy?* ☐

DAY 6 ———————————— *Date*
M T W T F S S

MOOD CHECK: *Cloudy?* ☐ OR *Happy?* ☐

DAY 7 ———————————— *Date*
M T W T F S S

MOOD CHECK: *Cloudy?* ☐ OR *Happy?* ☐

WEEK'S REVIEW

CLOUDY DAYS

SUNNY DAYS

TARGETS WON!

MY REWARD!

Give Yourself A Chance!

Week 2

"If Thomas Edison gave the lightbulb a 'Thousand Chances' at success, how many are you prepared to give yourself, when you're WORTH MORE than a lightbulb?!"

TARGET FOR THE WEEK

Less is more...!

ACTION PLANS

DAY 8 ———————————— *Date*
M T W T F S S

_____

_____
_____

_____

_____

MOOD CHECK: *Cloudy?* ☐ *OR* *Happy?* ☐

DAY 9 _____ Date
M T W T F S S

_____
_____
_____
_____
_____
_____

MOOD CHECK: Cloudy? ☐ OR Happy? ☐

DAY 10 _____ Date
M T W T F S S

_____
_____
_____
_____
_____
_____

MOOD CHECK: Cloudy? ☐ OR Happy? ☐

DAY 11 _____ Date
M T W T F S S

_____
_____
_____
_____
_____
_____

MOOD CHECK: Cloudy? ☐ OR Happy? ☐

DAY 12 ———————————— Date
M T W T F S S

MOOD CHECK: Cloudy? ☐ OR Happy? ☐

DAY 13 ———————————— Date
M T W T F S S

MOOD CHECK: Cloudy? ☐ OR Happy? ☐

DAY 14 ———————————— Date
M T W T F S S

MOOD CHECK: Cloudy? ☐ OR Happy? ☐

WEEK'S REVIEW

CLOUDY DAYS

SUNNY DAYS

TARGETS WON!

MY REWARD!

Set Your Own Expectations!

Week 3

"Quit living your life according to everyone's expectations. You have gifts, products and services that only YOU are QUALIFIED to share."

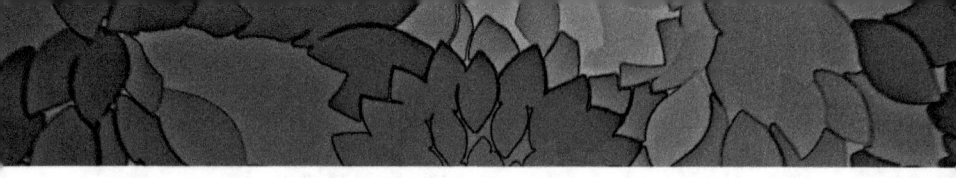

TARGET FOR THE WEEK

Less is more...!

ACTION PLANS

DAY 15 ———————————— *Date*
M T W F S S

———————————————————————
———————————————————————
———————————————————————
———————————————————————
———————————————————————

MOOD CHECK: Cloudy? ☐ OR Happy? ☐

DAY 16 ———————————— Date
M T W T F S S

_____

_____
_____

_____

_____

MOOD CHECK: Cloudy? ☐   OR   Happy? ☐

DAY 17 ———————————— Date
M T W T F S S

_____

_____
_____

_____

_____

MOOD CHECK: Cloudy? ☐   OR   Happy? ☐

DAY 18 ———————————— Date
M T W T F S S

_____

_____
_____

_____

_____

MOOD CHECK: Cloudy? ☐   OR   Happy? ☐

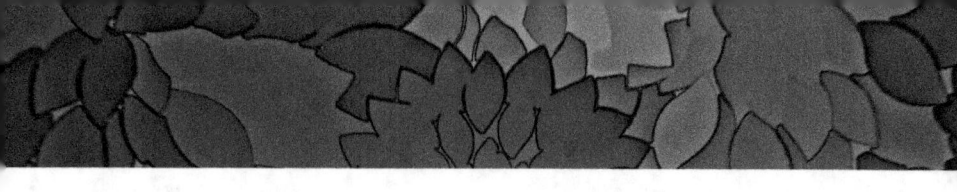

DAY 19 _____ Date
M T W T F S S

MOOD CHECK: Cloudy? ☐ OR Happy? ☐

DAY 20 _____ Date
M T W T F S S

MOOD CHECK: Cloudy? ☐ OR Happy? ☐

DAY 21 _____ Date
M T W T F S S

MOOD CHECK: Cloudy? ☐ OR Happy? ☐

WEEK'S REVIEW

CLOUDY DAYS

SUNNY DAYS

TARGETS WON!

MY REWARD!

You're On A Unique Life Path!

Week 4

"You have been uniquely
designed to play — YOU!
Your life, your circumstances,
your unfolding, and how you
navigate through life can never
be repeated."

TARGET FOR THE WEEK

Less is more...!

ACTION PLANS

DAY 22 ———————————— *Date*
M T W T F S S

_____

_____

_____

_____

MOOD CHECK: Cloudy? ☐ *OR Happy?* ☐

DAY 23 ———————————— Date
         M T W T F S S

MOOD CHECK: Cloudy? ☐   OR   Happy? ☐

DAY 24 ———————————— Date
         M T W T F S S

MOOD CHECK: Cloudy? ☐   OR   Happy? ☐

DAY 25 ———————————— Date
         M T W T F S S

MOOD CHECK: Cloudy? ☐   OR   Happy? ☐

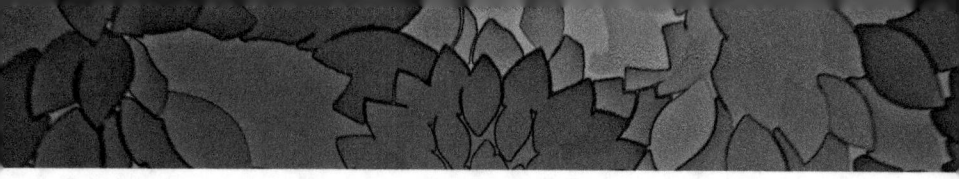

DAY 26 ———————————— Date
M T W T F S S

_____
_____
_____
_____
_____

MOOD CHECK: Cloudy? ☐ OR Happy? ☐

DAY 27 ———————————— Date
M T W T F S S

_____
_____
_____
_____
_____

MOOD CHECK: Cloudy? ☐ OR Happy? ☐

DAY 28 ———————————— Date
M T W T F S S

_____
_____
_____
_____
_____

MOOD CHECK: Cloudy? ☐ OR Happy? ☐

WEEK'S REVIEW

CLOUDY DAYS

SUNNY DAYS

TARGETS WON!

MY REWARD!

Go Easy On Yourself!

Week 5

"Some life experiences can be so strange, you'll question your sanity. There are things you may never understand and that's ok.

Go easy on yourself and do what you can."

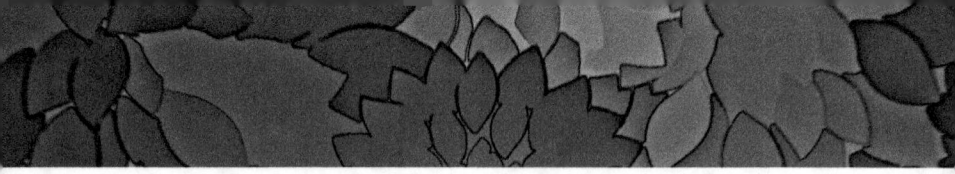

TARGET FOR THE WEEK

Less is more...!

ACTION PLANS

DAY 29 _____ *Date*
M T W T F S S

_____

_____

_____

_____

_____

MOOD CHECK: Cloudy? ☐   *OR   Happy?* ☐

DAY 30 ———————————— Date
M T W T F S S

_____
_____
_____
_____
_____

MOOD CHECK: Cloudy? ☐ OR Happy? ☐

DAY 31 ———————————— Date
M T W T F S S

_____
_____
_____
_____
_____

MOOD CHECK: Cloudy? ☐ OR Happy? ☐

DAY 32 ———————————— Date
M T W T F S S

_____
_____
_____
_____
_____

MOOD CHECK: Cloudy? ☐ OR Happy? ☐

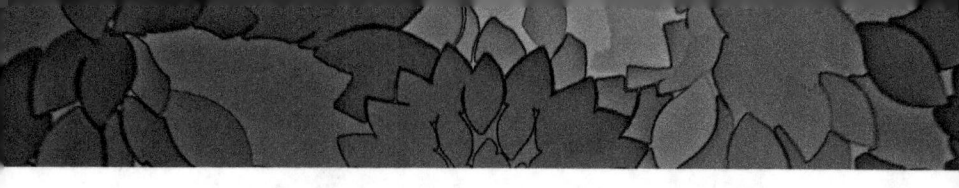

DAY 33 ———————— Date
M T W T F S S

_____
_____
_____
_____
_____

MOOD CHECK: *Cloudy?* ☐ OR *Happy?* ☐

DAY 34 ———————— Date
M T W T F S S

_____
_____
_____
_____
_____

MOOD CHECK: *Cloudy?* ☐ OR *Happy?* ☐

DAY 35 ———————— Date
M T W T F S S

_____
_____
_____
_____
_____

MOOD CHECK: *Cloudy?* ☐ OR *Happy?* ☐

WEEK'S REVIEW

CLOUDY DAYS

SUNNY DAYS

TARGETS WON!

MY REWARD!

Lose Not Your Sanity!

Week 6

"It's all Vanity
Have fun but...
Don't lose your Sanity."

TARGET FOR THE WEEK

Less is more...!

ACTION PLANS

DAY 36 _____ Date
M T W T F S S

_____
_____
_____
_____
_____

MOOD CHECK: Cloudy? ☐   OR   Happy? ☐

DAY 37 ———————————— *Date*
M T W T F S S

MOOD CHECK: *Cloudy?* ☐ OR *Happy?* ☐

DAY 38 ———————————— *Date*
M T W T F S S

MOOD CHECK: *Cloudy?* ☐ OR *Happy?* ☐

DAY 39 ———————————— *Date*
M T W T F S S

MOOD CHECK: *Cloudy?* ☐ OR *Happy?* ☐

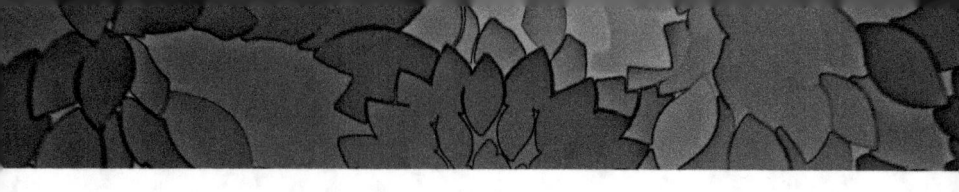

DAY 40 ———————— Date
M T W T F S S

_____
_____
_____
_____
_____

MOOD CHECK: *Cloudy?* ☐ OR *Happy?* ☐

DAY 41 ———————— Date
M T W T F S S

_____
_____
_____
_____
_____

MOOD CHECK: *Cloudy?* ☐ OR *Happy?* ☐

DAY 42 ———————— Date
M T W T F S S

_____
_____
_____
_____
_____

MOOD CHECK: *Cloudy?* ☐ OR *Happy?* ☐

WEEK'S REVIEW

CLOUDY DAYS

SUNNY DAYS

TARGETS WON!

MY REWARD!

Show up!

Week 7

"It's a new day
Go out - Take chances
You never know WHO or WHAT
may decide to show up
and blow your MIND!"

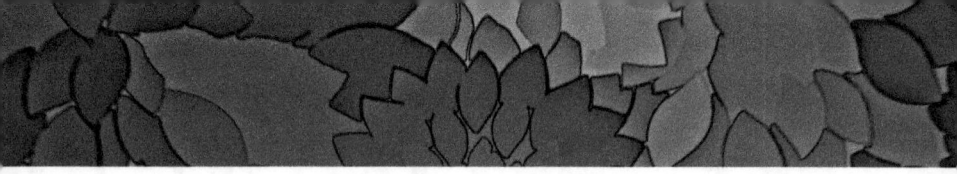

TARGET FOR THE WEEK

Less is more...!

DAY 43 ———————— *Date*
M T W T F S S

_____
_____
_____
_____
_____

MOOD CHECK: *Cloudy?* ☐ OR *Happy?* ☐

DAY 44 ———————————— Date
M T W T F S S

_____
_____
_____
_____
_____

MOOD CHECK: Cloudy? ☐ OR Happy? ☐

DAY 45 ———————————— Date
M T W T F S S

_____
_____
_____
_____
_____

MOOD CHECK: Cloudy? ☐ OR Happy? ☐

DAY 46 ———————————— Date
M T W T F S S

_____
_____
_____
_____
_____

MOOD CHECK: Cloudy? ☐ OR Happy? ☐

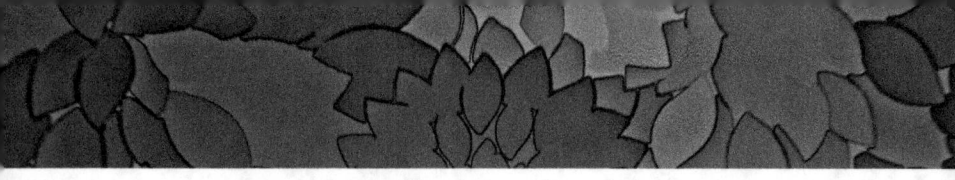

DAY 47 ———————————— Date
M T W T F S S

———————————————————————————
———————————————————————————
———————————————————————————
———————————————————————————

MOOD CHECK: Cloudy? ☐ OR Happy? ☐

DAY 48 ———————————— Date
M T W T F S S

———————————————————————————
———————————————————————————
———————————————————————————
———————————————————————————

MOOD CHECK: Cloudy? ☐ OR Happy? ☐

DAY 49 ———————————— Date
M T W T F S S

———————————————————————————
———————————————————————————
———————————————————————————
———————————————————————————

MOOD CHECK: Cloudy? ☐ OR Happy? ☐

WEEK'S REVIEW

CLOUDY DAYS

SUNNY DAYS

TARGETS WON!

MY REWARD!

Decide to DECIDE!

Week 8

"Never be discouraged
by troubled circumstances,
for they will soon pass
in a moment of DECISION
and appropriate ACTION."

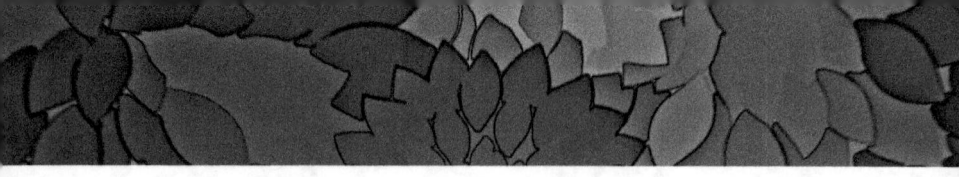

TARGET FOR THE WEEK

Less is more...!

ACTION PLANS

DAY 50   _____ *Date*
                                                       M T W T F S S

_____
_____
_____
_____
_____

MOOD CHECK: *Cloudy?* ☐   *OR*   *Happy?* ☐

DAY 51 ———————————— *Date*
M T W T F S S

_____

_____

_____

_____

_____

MOOD CHECK: *Cloudy?* ☐ *OR* *Happy?* ☐

DAY 52 ———————————— *Date*
M T W T F S S

_____

_____

_____

_____

_____

MOOD CHECK: *Cloudy?* ☐ *OR* *Happy?* ☐

DAY 53 ———————————— *Date*
M T W T F S S

_____

_____

_____

_____

_____

MOOD CHECK: *Cloudy?* ☐ *OR* *Happy?* ☐

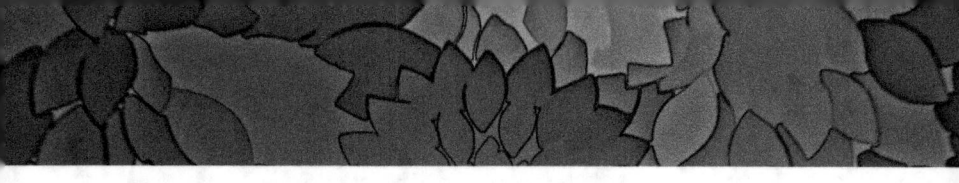

DAY 54 ———————————— Date
M T W T F S S

MOOD CHECK: Cloudy? ☐ OR Happy? ☐

DAY 55 ———————————— Date
M T W T F S S

MOOD CHECK: Cloudy? ☐ OR Happy? ☐

DAY 56 ———————————— Date
M T W T F S S

MOOD CHECK: Cloudy? ☐ OR Happy? ☐

WEEK'S REVIEW

CLOUDY DAYS

SUNNY DAYS

TARGETS WON!

MY REWARD!

Dare the Unknown!

Week 9

"Life is not like driving a car - where you'll need to see the end of the road before you emerge.

Venture into the unknown! Risk being drenched in the muddy-puddles of unknown TREASURES!"

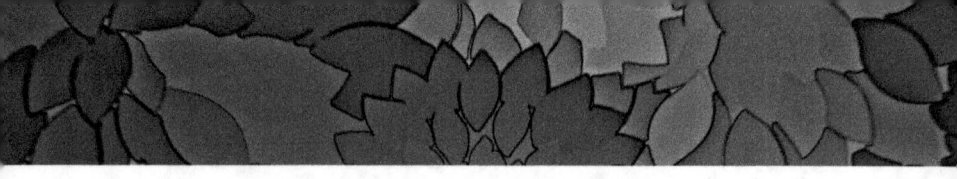

TARGET FOR THE WEEK

Less is more...!

ACTION PLANS

DAY 57 _____ *Date*
           M T W T F S S

_____
_____
_____
_____
_____

MOOD CHECK: Cloudy? ☐ *OR   Happy?* ☐

DAY 58 ———————————— *Date*
M T W T F S S

MOOD CHECK: Cloudy? ☐ OR Happy? ☐

DAY 59 ———————————— *Date*
M T W T F S S

MOOD CHECK: Cloudy? ☐ OR Happy? ☐

DAY 60 ———————————— *Date*
M T W T F S S

MOOD CHECK: Cloudy? ☐ OR Happy? ☐

DAY 61 ———————— Date
M T W T F S S

MOOD CHECK: Cloudy? ☐ OR Happy? ☐

DAY 62 ———————— Date
M T W T F S S

MOOD CHECK: Cloudy? ☐ OR Happy? ☐

DAY 63 ———————— Date
M T W T F S S

MOOD CHECK: Cloudy? ☐ OR Happy? ☐

WEEK'S REVIEW

CLOUDY DAYS

SUNNY DAYS

TARGETS WON!

MY REWARD!

Love With No Regrets!

Week 10

"LOVE...
The only mistake
worth making."

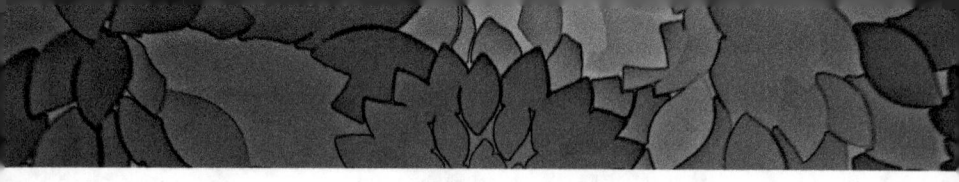

TARGET FOR THE WEEK

Less is more...!

ACTION PLANS

DAY 64   ———————— *Date*
                                                 M T W T F S S

_____

_____

_____

_____

_____

MOOD CHECK: Cloudy? ☐   OR   Happy? ☐

DAY 65 _____ *Date*
M T W T F S S

_____

_____

_____

_____

_____

MOOD CHECK: *Cloudy?* ☐ *OR* *Happy?* ☐

DAY 66 _____ *Date*
M T W T F S S

_____

_____

_____

_____

_____

MOOD CHECK: *Cloudy?* ☐ *OR* *Happy?* ☐

DAY 67 _____ *Date*
M T W T F S S

_____

_____

_____

_____

_____

MOOD CHECK: *Cloudy?* ☐ *OR* *Happy?* ☐

DAY 68 ———————————— *Date*
M T W T F S S

MOOD CHECK: *Cloudy?* ☐ OR *Happy?* ☐

DAY 69 ———————————— *Date*
M T W T F S S

MOOD CHECK: *Cloudy?* ☐ OR *Happy?* ☐

DAY 70 ———————————— *Date*
M T W T F S S

MOOD CHECK: *Cloudy?* ☐ OR *Happy?* ☐

WEEK'S REVIEW

CLOUDY DAYS

SUNNY DAYS

TARGETS WON!

MY REWARD!

Trust Your Inner Design!

Week 11

"Change not everything about you to FIT IN.

Sometimes, your difference is your Million Dollar DESIGN."

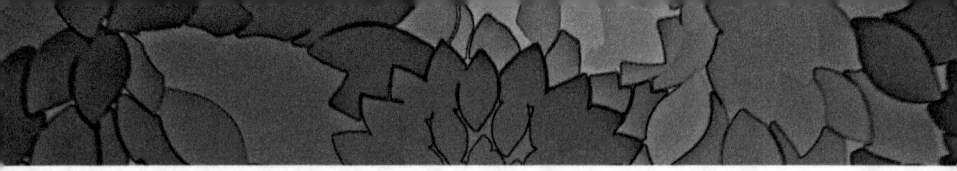

TARGET FOR THE WEEK

Less is more...!

ACTION PLANS

DAY 71 — — — — — — — — — — — *Date*
M T W T F S S

———————————————————————————
———————————————————————————
———————————————————————————
———————————————————————————
———————————————————————————

MOOD CHECK: *Cloudy?* ☐   OR   *Happy?* ☐

DAY 72 ———————————— Date
M T W T F S S

MOOD CHECK: Cloudy? ☐ OR Happy? ☐

DAY 73 ———————————— Date
M T W T F S S

MOOD CHECK: Cloudy? ☐ OR Happy? ☐

DAY 74 ———————————— Date
M T W T F S S

MOOD CHECK: Cloudy? ☐ OR Happy? ☐

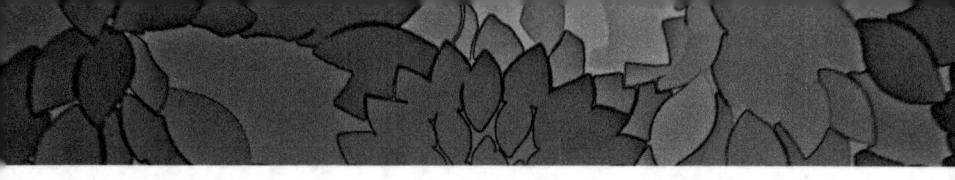

DAY 75 ———————— Date
M T W T F S S

_____
_____
_____
_____

MOOD CHECK: Cloudy? ☐ OR Happy? ☐

DAY 76 ———————— Date
M T W T F S S

_____
_____
_____
_____

MOOD CHECK: Cloudy? ☐ OR Happy? ☐

DAY 77 ———————— Date
M T W T F S S

_____
_____
_____
_____

MOOD CHECK: Cloudy? ☐ OR Happy? ☐

WEEK'S REVIEW

CLOUDY DAYS

SUNNY DAYS

TARGETS WON!

MY REWARD!

Release & Let It Go!

Week 12

"If your mind is not at ease,
then you, my friend,
are trying to please...
or worse, make peace
with what you must release.

Take the hint and let it go!"

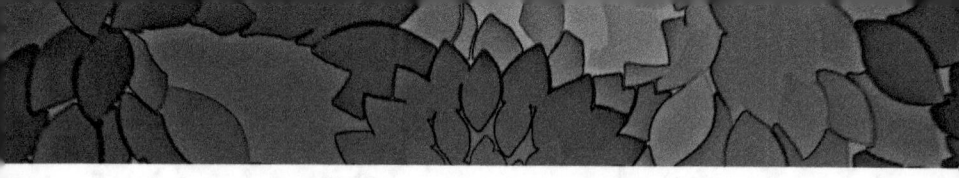

TARGET FOR THE WEEK

Less is more...!

ACTION PLANS

DAY 78   ——————— *Date*
                                                M T W T F S S

_____

_____

_____

_____

_____

MOOD CHECK: *Cloudy?* ☐   OR   *Happy?* ☐

DAY 79 —————————— Date
         M T W T F S S

MOOD CHECK: Cloudy? ☐ OR Happy? ☐

DAY 80 —————————— Date
         M T W T F S S

MOOD CHECK: Cloudy? ☐ OR Happy? ☐

DAY 81 —————————— Date
         M T W T F S S

MOOD CHECK: Cloudy? ☐ OR Happy? ☐

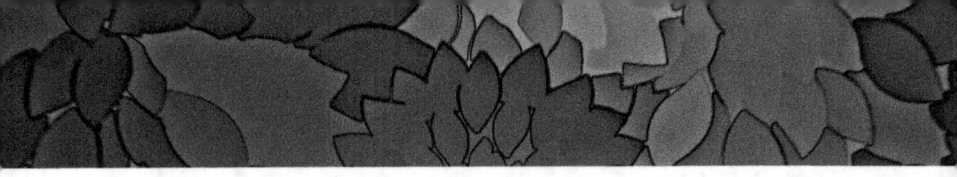

DAY 82 ———————————— Date
M T W T F S S

_____
_____
_____
_____
_____
_____

MOOD CHECK: Cloudy? ☐ OR Happy? ☐

DAY 83 ———————————— Date
M T W T F S S

_____
_____
_____
_____
_____
_____

MOOD CHECK: Cloudy? ☐ OR Happy? ☐

DAY 84 ———————————— Date
M T W T F S S

_____
_____
_____
_____
_____
_____

MOOD CHECK: Cloudy? ☐ OR Happy? ☐

WEEK'S REVIEW

CLOUDY DAYS

SUNNY DAYS

TARGETS WON!

MY REWARD!

You Can Do Anything!

Week Finale

"You made it this far
not because you're perfect
but because you chose to place
VALUE and INTEGRITY
upon yourself."

CONGRATULATIONS!!!

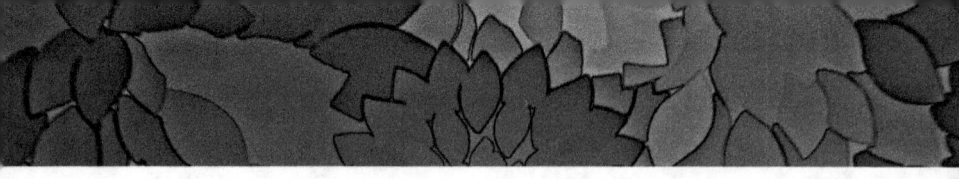

TARGET FOR THE WEEK

Less is more...!

ACTION PLANS

DAY 85 ———————— *Date*
M T W T F S S

———————————————————————
———————————————————————
———————————————————————
———————————————————————
———————————————————————

MOOD CHECK: Cloudy? ☐ *OR Happy?* ☐

DAY 86 ———————————— Date
M T W T F S S

MOOD CHECK: Cloudy? ☐ OR Happy? ☐

DAY 87 ———————————— Date
M T W T F S S

MOOD CHECK: Cloudy? ☐ OR Happy? ☐

DAY 88 ———————————— Date
M T W T F S S

MOOD CHECK: Cloudy? ☐ OR Happy? ☐

DAY 89 ———————— Date
M T W T F S S

MOOD CHECK: Cloudy? ☐   OR   Happy? ☐

DAY 90 ———————— Date
M T W T F S S

MOOD CHECK: Cloudy? ☐   OR   Happy? ☐

WEEK'S REVIEW

CLOUDY DAYS

SUNNY DAYS

TARGETS WON!

MY REWARD!

Date: ———————————

Notes

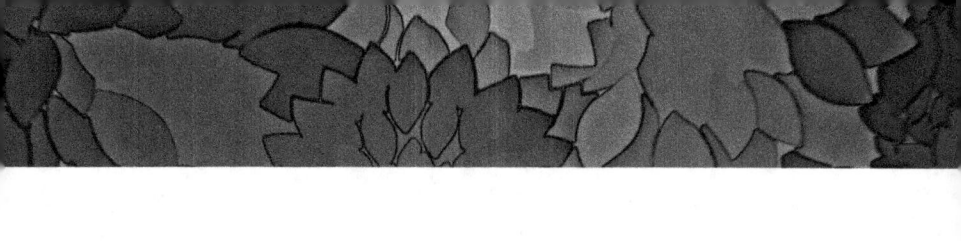

Date: ———————————

Notes

Date: ─────────────

Notes

Date: _____

Notes

Date: _____

Notes

Date: ———————

Notes

Date: _____

Notes

Date:

Notes

Date: ———————

Notes

Date: _____

Notes

Date: _____

Notes

Date: ―――――――

Notes

Date: ———————————

Notes

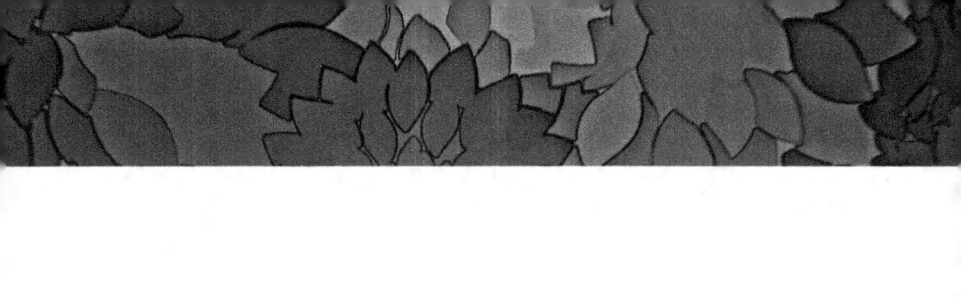

Date: ———————————

Notes

Date: ———————————

Notes

Date: ⎯⎯⎯⎯⎯⎯⎯⎯⎯⎯

Notes

Date: ───────────

Notes

Date: ─────────────

Notes

Date: _____

Notes

Date: ———————————

Notes

Date: ―――――――――

Notes

Date: ———————————

Notes

Date: ———————————

Notes

Date: ———————————

Notes

Date: ─────────────

Notes

Date: ───────────

Notes

Date:

Notes

Growth Companion Journal
- 90 DAYS OF BECOMING!
by Kamby Kamara

London, United Kingdom
Published by Growth Companion Journal Ltd.
www.kambykamara.com

Email: growthcompanions@yahoo.com

Copyright © 2020 by Kamby Kamara
First Edition 2019

All rights reserved worldwide.
No part of this publication may be replicated, redistributed, or given away in any form without the prior written consent of the author/publisher or the terms relayed to you herein.

www.ingramcontent.com/pod-product-compliance
Lightning Source LLC
Chambersburg PA
CBHW071451070526
44578CB00001B/298